Old Jokes for Old Folks

Aging with a Smile

Publications International, Ltd.

Holli Fort, having shared her adult life with four grandparents and one great-grandmother, can appreciate the wisdom and humor that comes with age. And as the mother of three young sons, she definitely needs it!

Angela Hampt-Sanchez is a mother of seven and the delighted grandmother of seven with two more grandchildren on the way. An extensive traveler, she makes sure that her sense of humor is always right at hand (keeping it in the car itself, not packed away in the trunk).

Finding themselves jobless in their early 60s, **Frank and Carolyn Kaiser** of Clearwater, Florida, began writing their international column, *Suddenly Senior*—the daily e-zine for everyone over 50 who feels way too young to be old. Eleven years later, it's read by 3.1 million in 83 newspapers and magazines around the world (www.suddenlysenior.com).

Comedy writer **Paul Seaburn** believes that laughter keeps him young, no matter what his driver's license photo implies. Paul writes comedy for television, radio, the Internet, humor books, magazines, and comedians. He's the head writer for a jazz-blues-and-comedy show on public radio and has more info and laughs at www.humorhandyman.com.

Illustrations: Shutterstock.com/Dennis Cox

Louis Weber, CEO
Publications International, Ltd.
8140 Lehigh Avenue
Morton Grove, Illinois 60053

Permission is never granted for commercial purposes.

ISBN-13: 978-1-4508-1716-5
ISBN-10: 1-4508-1716-5

Manufactured in U.S.A.

8 7 6 5 4 3 2 1

Contents

. . . .

The Years May Come, but the Fun Doesn't Have to Go!

. . . .

We all have to grow old, but that doesn't mean we have to grow up. If we did, we might not fully appreciate the hilarity involved in the process. *Old Jokes for Old Folks* is designed to help us all remember that although we may lose our hearing or agility, we never need to lose our sense of humor. From everyday situations to one-of-a-kind experiences, these jokes will remind you that even a brittle funny bone needs to be tickled every once in a while.

It's My Party, and I'll Nap If I Want To

. . . .

To make conversation during the bridge game, Emma asked, "Hey, have you all seen those new soap operas for seniors?"

"Oh, yes," said Grace. "I'm a big fan of *As the Rocker Creaks.*"

"Really?" replied Emma. "I thought that one was okay, but there's a lot more action on *(Last) Days of Our Lives!*"

* * *

Charlie's doctor told him that he was only allowed one drink a day. He asked his friend the veterinarian if he agreed with that, and he did. So now Charlie has seven drinks a day, because it's only one each in dog days.

* * *

Horace was, as usual, up to his old complaints.

"If you ask me, these young kids with all of their pierced ears and noses and tongues and other places have ruined going to the beach with a metal detector."

*   *   *

*Age is a very high price
to pay for maturity.*

—TOM STOPPARD

*   *   *

A little old lady was sitting on a park bench in Miami Beach when a man walked over and sat down on the other end of the bench. After a few moments, the woman asked, "Are you a stranger here?"

The man replied, "I used to live here many years ago."

"So, where have you been all these years?"

"In prison," he said.

"Why were you in prison?"

He looked at her and very quietly said, "I killed my wife."

"Oh," said the woman. "So you're single…"

*   *   *

Who needs energy drinks? At Sophie's age, she can keep herself awake for five hours just by talking about her grandkids.

*   *   *

THE BRIGHT SIDES OF AGING

· · · · · · · · · · · · · · · · · · · ·

- Less peer pressure
- No penalty for IRA withdrawals
- Nothing left to learn the hard way
- No time for procrastinating

You Must Be Bluffing

Jill looked up in amusement as her husband finally wandered into the kitchen at 11:30 in the morning. Since they'd both retired, he hadn't exactly been keeping what she'd call "office hours."

"You must have been on quite a streak last night at the casino to get home so late! Were you winning or losing?"

"I wasn't out that late!" protested her husband.

"Losing, then," said Jill.

"No, really, I wasn't out that late. You were just sleeping very, very soundly by the time I got in."

"Well," Jill replied, "then I guess I'll have to tell the paper boy to stop delivering the paper under the front wheel of your car!"

* * *

Mysterious Ways

Jack was obsessed with fishing and spent most of his retirement doing just that, but he promised his wife that he wouldn't fish during their weeklong trip. A few days in, though, he just couldn't take it anymore. On Sunday morning, he told his wife he was sick, waited until she left for church, and then headed out to a nearby lake to rent a boat and some gear. Right away, he caught a fish that was bigger than any he'd ever seen.

Once they were back at home, Jack went to confession and told the priest all that had happened. "Father," he said, "there's one thing I don't understand. Why would God reward me with a big fish when he should have punished me for lying and skipping church?"

"He did punish you!" laughed the priest. "Who are you going to tell about it?"

* * *

When people tell you how young you look, they are also telling you how old you are.

—CARY GRANT

* * *

The band the Village People are out touring again, after so many years. They have a new hit single:

"It's Fun to Play for the A-A-R-P!"

* * *

When I was a teenager and a pretty girl looked at me, I thought I was hot stuff.

When I was middle-aged and a pretty girl looked at me, I thought, "Not bad for a guy my age."

Now when a pretty girl looks at me, I think I better make sure my fly is zipped.

* * *

A pair of retired men got together for a walk around the lake. Bill announced that he had gotten engaged to his 30-something girlfriend. Perturbed, George said, "Well, Bill, you know that age difference is no good for you. I'm sorry to do it, but I just have to tell it like it is."

"I used to believe the exact same thing," Bill replied. "But that was before I had a 30-something girlfriend!"

*   *   *

You know you're getting old when your "can-do" spirit turns into "wish I could" spirit.

* * *

It is well for the world that in most of us, by the age of 30, the character has been set like plaster, and will never soften again.

—WILLIAM JAMES

* * *

Q & A
· · · · ·

Q. Why is it that it's so much easier to get along with your grandkids than it was to get along with your kids when they were a similar age?

A. Because you and your grandkids have the same opponent!

A man in his 80s got up and put on his coat. His wife asked, "Where are you going?"

He said, "I'm going to the doctor."

"Are you sick?" she replied.

"No" he said, "I'm going to get me some of those new Viagra pills." So his wife got out of her rocker and put on *her* coat, as well.

He said, "And where are you going?"

"I'm going to the doctor, too," she said.

"Why?" he asked.

She said, "If you're going to start using that rusty old thing, I'm going to get me a tetanus shot."

✳　✳　✳

Old night owls never die, they just don't give a hoot if they get out anymore.

✳　✳　✳

Two elderly men were sunning themselves in Palm Springs when they started a friendly conversation.

"I was able to move here to retire in Palm Springs after my business burned to the ground," the one man said. "The insurance payment sure came in handy."

The other replied, "I'm here living on an insurance payout from when my factory was flooded out."

The first man pondered for a few seconds and then asked, "How do you start a flood?"

* * *

Grandma had to talk fast to get out of a speeding ticket the other day. She explained to the officer that if she didn't drive fast, she'd forget where she was going before she got there.

* * *

I don't know how you feel about old age ... but in my case I didn't even see it coming. It hit me from the rear.

—PHYLLIS DILLER

* * *

Ferdinand told the grandkids he was going to teach them how to can tomatoes, but they assured him they already knew how. The kids lined the tomatoes up on the counter, walked over to each one, and said, "You're fired!"

* * *

Since You're Going Right By...

While on vacation, an elderly couple had driven quite some distance from the diner they had stopped in for lunch before the wife realized she'd left her prescription reading glasses at the table. Her husband moaned and groaned all the way back to the restaurant. The poor woman really felt bad for annoying her husband so much, but as she was getting out of the car at the diner, he said to her, "Well, as long as you're going back in there, you might as well get my wallet, too. I must have left it by the cash register."

*   *   *

During their regular Senior Step class, Jan turned to Laura and said, "You know, I've always admired your great attitude. You never let anything get you down."

"Of course not," Laura laughed. "At my age, I might never get back up!"

*   *   *

An older motorcycle rider was stopped at a light at a crossroads one midnight. In a puff of smoke and a roar that drowned out the motorcycle engine, the devil appeared. Everyone in the area raced away in terror. Everyone, that is, but the old biker.

"Don't you know who I am?" the devil asked.

"Of course, I do. You're Satan."

"And that doesn't frighten you?"

"Why would it?" the biker replied. "I've been married to your sister for 45 years."

Thelma: "Did I ever tell you about my grandchildren?"

Mabel: "No, and I appreciate that."

✳   ✳   ✳

Careful grooming may take 20 years off a woman's age, but you can't fool a long flight of stairs.

—MARLENE DIETRICH

✳   ✳   ✳

After experiencing yet another computer glitch, Barb called her son over to troubleshoot.

"Mom," he said, "I keep telling you—you have to back up your hard drive!"

"I would, Son," Barb replied, "if you would just show me how to put the damned thing in reverse!"

✳   ✳   ✳

His Eternal Reward

After a life of penny-pinching, Jim had amassed a great wealth, but he was terrified of losing it, so he spent as little as possible. Then a doctor told him that he had a terminal illness.

"Jim," advised the doctor, "it's time to live it up. Use your last few weeks to travel with Cathy, do all the things you always wanted to do."

But Jim was stubborn and greedy, so instead, he cashed in every stock or bond he owned, closed all of his bank accounts, and put all of the money in a box. As the end drew near, he made one final demand on his wife: She must bury all the money with him. After much back-and-forth, she reluctantly agreed to his last wish.

At the funeral, Cathy placed the box at Jim's right hand. Her best friend whispered to her, "Are you crazy? How could you give up all that money?"

"Well," Cathy grinned, "I didn't feel like it was safe for him to be buried with all that cash, so I deposited it in my account for safekeeping and wrote the stingy old jerk a check!"

*   *   *

I don't let old age bother me. There are three signs of old age. Loss of memory...I forget the other two.

—RED SKELTON

*   *   *

Alfred always thought life insurance was an odd gamble. "The insurance company bets you'll live. You bet you won't, and you invest a fortune backing up that wager. But when it's all said and done, you end up pulling for the company to be right."

*   *   *

One day Danny was surprised to see a police car pull up to the house. The officer got out and came around to help Danny's elderly father out of the backseat. The officer guided him by the arm over to Danny.

"Dad, what is it?" Danny asked anxiously. "What in the world is wrong?" He looked to the officer, who was the first to speak.

"Your father was lost in the park. He had his ID with him, so I thought I'd better bring him home."

After the officer left, the father let Danny in on a little secret: "I wasn't exactly lost. I was just too tired to walk home."

*   *   *

"It's not so bad having shaky hands," Agnes explained. "Now when I'm at the grocery store and pushing the shopping cart, the wheels stop wobbling."

*   *   *

Hokey Pokey

With all the sadness and trauma going on in the world at the moment, it is worth reflecting on the death of a very important person. Larry La Prise, the man who wrote "The Hokey Pokey," died peacefully at age 93.

The most traumatic part for his family was getting him into the coffin. They put his left foot in, and that's when the trouble started.

*   *   *

The best way to get most husbands to do something is to suggest that perhaps they're too old to do it.

—ANNE BANCROFT

* * *

A lady went to the bar on a cruise ship and ordered a scotch with two drops of water. As the bartender gave her the drink she said, "I'm on this cruise to celebrate my 80th birthday, and it's today."

The bartender answered, "Well, since it's your birthday, I'll buy you a drink. In fact, this one's on me."

As the woman finished her drink, a woman to her right said, "I'd like to buy you a drink, too."

Pleased, the old woman said, "Thank you. Bartender, I want a scotch with two drops of water."

As she finished that drink, a man to her left said, "You know what? I'd like to buy you one, too." The old woman thanked him and once again ordered scotch with two drops of water.

As he gave her the drink, the bartender wondered aloud. "Ma'am, I'm dying of curiosity. Why the scotch with only two drops of water?"

The old woman replied, "Sonny, when you're my age, you've learned how to hold your liquor. Holding your water, however, is a whole other issue."

* * *

There's a new auto parts store that caters to seniors.

If you're over 65, they throw in a free replacement for burned-out turn signals.

*　　*　　*

After decades of wearing her signature scent, Alice learned that it had been discontinued by the manufacturer. So off she went to the nearest department store to find a new fragrance.

She perused the selection: *Obsession, Romance, Desire, Passion.*

"Excuse me," she said to the saleslady, "but I just got out of a long-term relationship with a perfume. This time I just want something to make me smell nice!"

"No problem," said the clerk, not missing a beat, and handed Alice a bottle of *Fling.*

*　　*　　*

An elderly man went in to see his doctor to report that he had given up wine, women, and song. "How many years," he asked, "will this stark deprivation add to my life?"

"None really," replied his doctor. "Every year will just seem longer."

* * *

EAGLES SONGS FOR SENIORS

- New Geezer in Town
- Retirement Village California
- Peaceful Easy Bowel Movement
- Prune Juice and Tequila Sunrise
- Hard Ache Tonight
- Life in the Fast Lane with Your Blinker On
- Which Woman?
- One of These Nights I'm Not Going to Have to Go to the Bathroom

Things are much more advanced now than they were in my day. I got a new microwave TV. Now I can watch a one-hour show in nine minutes.

*　*　*

I'm growing old by myself. My wife hasn't had a birthday in years.

—MILTON BERLE

*　*　*

At her age, she looks like a million bucks... all green and crumply.

*　*　*

Doris was getting disgusted with how Felix was spending his retirement. "You're so involved with golf that I bet you don't even remember the day we got married."

"Sure, I do," Felix replied. "It was that beautiful afternoon I sank a 40-foot putt."

On their way to water aerobics class, Hildy and Anne repeated their most inspirational motto: "First, the buns of steel; then, the buns of cinnamon."

* * *

Frank was an outdoorsman, active in many sports, and never sick a day in his life. Why, he was even skiing well into his 80s, but then he started to go downhill real fast.

* * *

A tour bus driver was driving a bus full of seniors down a highway, when a little old lady tapped him on his shoulder. She offered him a handful of almonds, which he gratefully munched up. After approximately 15 minutes, she tapped him on the shoulder again and handed him another handful of almonds.

She repeated this gesture about eight times. Finally, the bus driver asked her why the seniors didn't eat the almonds themselves. She told him that it was impossible because of their old teeth. They weren't able to chew them.

"Why do you buy them at all, then?" he asked, puzzled.

"We just love the chocolate around them."

*   *   *

You know you're old when you no longer have a list of places that are open all night.

*   *   *

Pansy always said, "A great thing about being our age is that your secrets are safe with your friends. They can't remember them long enough to repeat them."

*   *   *

Who needs rock walls when you can get the same excitement just climbing onto a stool?

*   *   *

There were two lines leading into heaven. Over one was a sign that read, "Henpecked Husbands," and there was no end in sight for that line. The other line had a sign that read "Real He-Men," but only one little old man was standing there. St. Peter walked over to the little gent and asked him why he was standing there. The little old man answered meekly, "Because my wife told me to."

*   *   *

A little old lady who was quite the tart in her day was known for wandering around the halls of her nursing home. Whenever she approached a man, she did a little dance, flipped up the hem of her dress, and said, "Supersex."

She never had any takers, though. In fact, no men even spoke back to her at all, until one day a fellow glanced up at her from his wheelchair and said, "Well, thank you! I'll have the soup, please!"

*　　*　　*

After 30, a body has a mind of its own.

—BETTE MIDLER

*   *   *

Max: "I bought this great *Brain Games* book of puzzles that are supposed to improve my memory."

Gus: "Really? How's that going?"

Max: "I'm sure it would be very helpful, if I could only remember where the heck I put the thing!"

*   *   *

Barney's pastor gives a special sermon when most of the congregation is made up of seniors. It's titled "Blessed Are the Pacemakers."

*   *   *

A woman came home to find that her husband had had a car accident while he was still in the garage.

"What happened? Did you forget to open the garage door before you backed out again?"

"Of course I didn't!" There was a long pause, then he admitted in a small voice, "But I did forget to close the car door."

*   *   *

Ernest reads all the recalls that the government announces . . . just in case they discontinue his blood type.

*   *   *

By the time a man is wise enough to watch his step, he's too old to go anywhere.

—BILLY CRYSTAL

*   *   *

You know you're old when you start singing along with the elevator music.

*   *   *

Why does everyone at the doctor's office ask how "we" are until it's time to pay the bill?

*   *   *

Herman knew he was old when he got a birthday call from NASA saying the astronauts saw his cake from the space station.

*   *   *

Q & A
· · · · ·

Q: Why did the granny cross the road?

A: To shut up the annoying Boy Scout.

Watch It—There's Still Time to Change My Will

. . . .

Brian and Melissa stopped at their mom's house for a surprise visit. When she answered the door, she was very flushed and sweaty. They immediately started to panic. "Mom, are you all right? What happened?"

"Oh, hello, dears. I've just been doing a DVD workout. I just love that Jane Fonda!"

"You were exercising? When did you start doing that?"

"Well, I figured at my age, this is the only way I get to hear some heavy breathing!"

*   *   *

Clara says that now that she's older, she's sleeping just like a baby again—up every two hours, and spending most of the night in the rocking chair.

*   *   *

You know you look old when you run into an old schoolmate at the grocery store and say, "I think you were in my class!" and she replies, "Really? Are you still teaching there?"

*   *   *

A Fourth Wish?

An old woman saved a fairy's life and was then granted three wishes. For the first wish, the old woman asked to become young and beautiful. Poof, she became young and beautiful.

For the second wish, the old woman asked to be the richest woman in the world. Poof, she was the richest woman in the world.

For the last wish, the now lovely, young woman pointed at her faithful companion, an old house cat, and requested that he be turned into the most handsome young man on earth. Poof, the wish was granted, and the fairy bid her fond farewell.

After the fairy left, the handsome man strolled over to the beautiful woman and snarled, "Now, aren't you sorry you had me neutered?"

*   *   *

Always read something that will make you look good if you die in the middle of it.

—P. J. O'ROURKE

*   *   *

It used to be that I had a mind like a steel trap.

Now it's more like a steel trap*door.*

*   *   *

Q & A
· · · · ·

Q: What's the fastest way to get five old ladies to swear a blue streak?

A: Get a sixth old lady to call out, "Bingo!"

When I was a boy the Dead Sea was only sick.

—GEORGE BURNS

* * *

Call Me

While visiting, Amanda found her mother's little black book. She took a peek inside and was shocked at how many men's names and numbers there were. She decided to confront her mother: "Mother! Surely you aren't seeing all of these men."

"Sometimes," Cathy replied serenely. "A few of them I see fairly regularly."

"But . . . but . . . but . . . at your age?"

"What do you have to be so offended about? As a teenager, you always said that you should be able to see whoever you wanted to and it was nobody else's business. Why should it be any different for me at my age?" Cathy asked, as she sailed out of the room.

Baffled, Amanda decided to call one of the numbers. After a few rings, a chipper voice answered: "Dr. Alexander's office. How can I help you?"

* * *

At Jonah's age, "Texas Hold 'Em" is a pair of suspenders he got in El Paso.

* * *

The Rolling Stones are still touring, which is great, really. Mick Jagger sometimes gets a little confused, though, and sings about how he really feels, rather than the actual lyrics. "I'm Jumping Jack Flash, I've Got Gas, Gas, Gas…"

*   *   *

"Now that I'm 80," Jack said, "people keep teasing me about being over the hill."

"So what's the problem?" asked Earl.

"I can't remember ever being on *top* of the hill!"

*   *   *

The Retirement Center Prayer

Grant me the senility to forget the people here I don't like, the good fortune to run into the ones that I do, and the eyesight to notice the difference.

*   *   *

Best Friends Forever

Two old men had been meeting in the park to play chess for years. One day, Frank finally confessed to Henry: "I must really be having a senior moment—all of the sudden, I can't think of your name. Help me out?"

After a long and extremely tense pause came his friend's reply: "I'll have to get back to you on that one."

* * *

By my rambling digressions I perceive myself to be growing older.

—BENJAMIN FRANKLIN

* * *

You know you're old when you have to get a stretch medicine cabinet.

* * *

I'm at that age when I put on a belt *and* suspenders even when I'm wearing a jumpsuit.

* * *

The Way to His Heart

Before Beth got married, her mother advised her to always have a stockpile of frozen meals that she could just heat up for dinner when her husband got home. But since he never requested any of the various roasts and casseroles and pot pies she had so lovingly prepared, Beth had been forced to adjust. Now she has a whole freezer filled with carefully labeled containers bearing the name of one of her husband's top five dinner requests: *Whatever You Want, Anything, Something Good, I Don't Know,* and *Food.*

* * *

You know you're getting old when you take mountain-climbing lessons to get into bed.

* * *

Simon decided that this was the last year he would have candles on his birthday cake. They'd left so much wax on his cake, it had a nicer shine than his head.

✳   ✳   ✳

It says in the Book of Genesis that Adam lived to be 900 years old. That explains why Eve ate the apple and they had to put on clothes. Nobody wants to see a 900-year-old man naked.

✳   ✳   ✳

The "Yokes" on the Restaurant

An elderly couple went to breakfast at a restaurant where the "seniors' special" was two eggs, bacon, hash browns, and toast for $1.99.

"Sounds good," the woman said. "But I don't want the eggs."

"Then I'll have to charge you $2.49 because you're ordering à la carte," the waitress warned her.

"Wait a minute," the woman said, amazed. "You mean I'd have to pay 50 cents for *not* taking the eggs? Then, I'll have the special."

"How do you want your eggs?"

"I'll have the eggs on the side, please," the woman replied. "Raw and in the shell."

The couple enjoyed their breakfast very much. When they finished, the woman put her two eggs in her purse and went home.

✳   ✳   ✳

What a wonderful life I've had!
I only wish I'd realized it sooner.

—COLETTE

BOARD GAMES FOR SENIORS

• •

- Monopoly of the Conversation by Talking About My Grandkids
- Lack of Concentration
- Sugar-Free Candy Land
- Cottagecheesi
- Don't Break the Wind
- Tic-Tac-Toe Fungus
- Shoots—My Bladder
- Talk About My Operation
- I'll Give You Something to Be Sorry About
- The Game of Life? Let Me Tell You About Life

At 83 years old, George went for his annual physical. All of his tests came back with normal results. Dr. Smith said, "George, everything looks great. How's everything with your wife?"

George replied, "Yeah, my wife and I are doing very well. She's even made it easier for me during my trips to the bathroom in the middle of the night. Somehow she's fixed something up so that when I open the bathroom door—*poof*—the light goes on. And when I'm done and I close the door—*poof*—the light goes off."

"Wow!" commented Dr. Smith, "that's incredible! She must be very inventive."

A little later in the day, Dr. Smith called George's wife. "Ethel," he said, "George is doing fine. Physically he's great. But I had to call because I'm impressed with what you've set up for him. Is it true that he gets up during the night and—*poof*—the light goes on in the bathroom, and then when he is through—*poof*—the light goes off?"

"Oh, no," Ethel exclaimed. "He's peeing in the refrigerator again!"

*   *   *

If you convince your tightwad old friend to finally spend some money and go visit a massage parlor, would that be considered contributing to the delinquency of a miser?

*   *   *

Thomas Jefferson once said, "We should never judge a president by his age, only by his works." And ever since he told me that, I stopped worrying.

—RONALD REAGAN

* * *

An elderly couple was attending church services. About halfway through the sermon, the husband leaned over and said, "I just let out a silent fart. What do you think I should do?"

The wife replied, "Put a new battery in your hearing aid."

* * *

You know you're getting old when you begin to wish rocking chairs were battery operated.

* * *

The technicians who design hearing aids must not be very old. You can tell, because their models don't come with filters for "rap music," "spouse," or "neighbor's dog."

* * *

It's not surprising that some people wait until they're 80 to take up skydiving. If you're going to have your life flash before your eyes, at least it will be a longer trip.

* * *

You know you're getting old when it takes you the whole night to do something you used to do the whole night through.

* * *

I'm at that age when a little wine helps me fall asleep. Especially when my wife is whining that she can't fall asleep.

* * *

"**G**randma, doesn't it bother you when people make fun of your age on your birthday?"

"No, dear. I just take it with a grain of salt... a bite of lime, and a shot of tequila!"

* * *

She Was Packing Heat, I Tell You!

A little old lady comes out of the mall. As she is nearly to her car, she sees four young men opening the doors and getting in.

"No you don't!" she yells, pulling a small pistol from her purse. Determined not to be intimidated, she waves it at the fellow in the driver's seat.

The four guys jump out of the car and run off.

When the old lady gets into her car, she can't understand why her keys don't fit. Finally, she realizes she's in the wrong car and gets out to find her own. In the correct car, she drives

straight to the police station to report the four guys who were trying to steal someone else's car. Much to her delight, she discovers that the police have been doing their job, and the four would-be car thieves are already in custody. As she nears the desk sergeant, she hears one of them shouting, "You have to believe us, officer! A little old lady just pulled a gun on us and stole our car!"

* * *

Definition of "indentured servant": senior working part-time to pay for false teeth.

The elderly cowboy watched as the auto mechanic very carefully examined his car. After a few minutes, he came back and said, "Sir, I'll give you terms you can understand. If your car were a horse, I'd shoot it."

If wrinkles must be written upon our brows, let them not be written upon the heart. The spirit should never grow old.

—JAMES A. GARFIELD

*   *   *

You know you're old when your boyfriend gets excited when he sees your panty lines and you aren't wearing any.

*   *   *

Q & A

Q: How many senior citizens does it take to screw in a lightbulb?

A: None. Don't worry about me. I'll just sit here in the dark.

Richard had 50-yard-line tickets for the Super Bowl. As he sat down in his seat, a man came down and asked him if anyone had the seat next to him.

"No," Richard said. "The seat is empty."

"This is incredible," said the man. "Who in their right mind would have a seat like this for the Super Bowl, the biggest sports event in the world, and not use it?"

Somberly, Richard replied, "Well...the seat actually belongs to me. I was supposed to come here with my wife, but she passed away. We got married in 1967, and this is my first Super Bowl without her."

"Oh, I'm sorry to hear that. That's terrible. But couldn't you find someone else—a friend or relative—to take the seat?"

Richard shakes his head, "No. They're all at her funeral."

* * *

I guess I don't mind so much being old, as I mind being fat and old.

—PETER GABRIEL

* * *

You know you're old when your barber offers you a lifetime guarantee.

* * *

John took his grandson along to the grocery store one day. The boy chattered nonstop until he got to a question that thoroughly stumped him:

"Grandpa, where do the coupons go after we use them?"

"I don't know, Bobby," replied Grandpa. "Where do you think they go?"

"Heaven?" asked Bobby.

"Only the redeemed ones," replied Grandpa.

$$* \quad * \quad *$$

You know you're a senior when you avoid Jell-O because it's too tough to chew and shakes less than you do.

$$* \quad * \quad *$$

A Win-Win Situation

On the verge of retirement, a lawyer found himself wistfully thinking back over his

career and wishing he was young and vibrant again.

"If I were just starting out now, I could use all of this technology and really make a killing!" he thought.

Suddenly, the devil appeared and offered him a bargain: The lawyer could be young again with his legal career in front of him while still retaining all the knowledge he had as an old man. In return, the devil would demand his soul for eternity.

The lawyer thought about it for a moment, then replied:

"Okay... but there's got to be a catch."

$$* \quad * \quad *$$

Edward got fired on his first day on the job as a store greeter. He kept yelling at the people parking cars in front to get off of his lawn.

$$* \quad * \quad *$$

Three lifelong Chicago Cubs fans got together a while back for their annual trip to Wrigley Field. To spur on the lovable losers, the women each held a sign. Put together, they read: "Cubs in '08—We Are Too Old to Wait!"

* * *

Our Sunday Drive

Two dear old friends took turns every Sunday driving around the town where they had grown up. As they were cruising along, they came to an intersection. Although the light turned red, they rolled right on through. The passenger thought to herself, "Well, it must have been safe, I suppose."

At the very next light, the exact same thing happened, only this time they had a narrow miss with another car! The passenger was sure they were in the wrong but wasn't certain what to say.

At the very next intersection, the light was red even before they got to it, but her friend drove right through again, just as she had the other two. This time the woman in the passenger seat had had enough. "Stella, you just ran three red lights in a row! You could have killed us both!" Stella turned to her and said, "Oh, my! Am I driving?"

✳   ✳   ✳

The aging process has you firmly in its grasp if you never get the urge to throw a snowball.

—DOUG LARSON

✳ ✳ ✳

Mabel had a pain beneath her right breast that was really bothering her. She finally went to the doctor to find out what it was. It turned out she had arthritis in her knee.

✳ ✳ ✳

Q & A
· · · · ·

Q: What do you call six guys at a funeral who are upset because the deceased looks better than they do?

A: Appalled bearers.

You know you're old when there's more fiber in your cereal than in your rugs.

* * *

They Worked Like a Charm

I took my elderly mother in for her checkup, during which she mentioned feeling very sluggish. Her doctor looked at all her lab results then left the room and returned with three bottles of large pills. His instructions were that my mother should take two red pills in the morning, two blue pills in the afternoon, two green pills in the evening, and return in one month. It was crucial, the doctor noted, that the pills be taken with two large glasses of water for each two pills.

When I returned with my mother to her doctor, she was feeling much better, and I took the opportunity of her using the restroom to ask him about the medication she was using. "Oh, just placebos—no one listens to me when I tell them to drink more water!"

* * *

You know you're getting old when you attach a cord to your cordless phone because you're tired of looking for it.

*   *   *

IF THEY DESIGNED DOGS FOR SENIORS, WE'D HAVE:

- Remote Control Retriever
- Boredom Collie
- A Good Shih Tzu
- Retaining Water Spaniel
- Losing My Hairdale
- Belching Shepherd
- Iron Poor Bloodhound
- Shorts Pinscher
- Shopping Maltese
- Peeingese

The Memorial Stone

A woman lost her husband, who had $30,000 to his name.

After everything had been finished at the funeral home and cemetery, she told her closest friend that there was none of the $30,000 left.

"How can that be?" the friend asked.

The widow thought, and said, "Well, the funeral cost me $6,500. And of course I made a donation to the church, for $500. And I spent another $500 for the wake, food, and drinks, you know. The rest went for the memorial stone."

The friend was astonished. "$22,500 for the memorial stone? My God, how big is it?"

The widow replied, "Three carats."

* * *

How do you spot an old optimist? His glass is half full of teeth.

Doctor: "How's your sex life now that you've retired?

Patient: "To tell you the truth, doctor, it's a lot like my Social Security check."

Doctor: "What do you mean?"

Patient: "Well, it's nice to get a little something, but it doesn't go nearly far enough."

*   *   *

Jonas was a minister for over 50 years, but last year he was put out to pastor.

*   *   *

I'm taking Viagra and drinking prune juice—I don't know if I'm coming or going!

—RODNEY DANGERFIELD

Do Senior Discounts Make Getting Old Worthwhile?

. . . .

Betsy's grandma's really old, but she hasn't slowed down too much. The family had to have an airbag installed in her walker for safety.

✳　　✳　　✳

Over lunch, Martha confessed to her best friend, Anna, that she was thinking of having Botox injections to look younger.

"Oh, Martha, don't do it! I tried it, and it really is the worst thing you could do."

"But Anna, you look so happy...."

"Exactly! I'm frowning with all my might at you right now."

✳　　✳　　✳

*She said she was approaching 40,
and I couldn't help wondering
from what direction.*

—BOB HOPE

*   *   *

COCKTAILS FOR SENIORS

- Gin and Panic
- Long Island Lukewarm Tea
- Sleep on the Beach
- Iron-Poor Bloody Mary
- Fuzzy Vision
- Gin Fizzed Out
- Mai Tai Has Another Stain
- Hairy Buffalo Ears
- Alabama Slamma Grandma
- Milk of Amnesia

He's so old that when they lit the candles on his cake someone yelled out, "Let the Olympic Games begin!"

* * *

Mr. Johnson had a strange feeling: He was experiencing amnesia and déjà vu at the same time. Whatever it was he'd just forgotten, he felt sure that he'd forgotten it before.

* * *

Erin had been seeing the same doctor for years. He had done her appendectomy, her gallbladder surgery, even her hysterectomy. One day, she went to see him because she thought she had tonsillitis. He took one look at her chart and said, "I've had just about enough out of you!"

*　　*　　*

When you get to a "certain age," it can really be hard to make ends meet. There are some months when I can't even get them to wave to each other across the street.

*　　*　　*

Two old guys were pushing their carts around the department store when they collided. The first old guy said to the second, "Sorry about that. I'm looking for my wife, and I guess I wasn't paying attention to where I was going."

The second old guy said, "That's okay. It's a coincidence. I'm looking for my wife, too, and I can't find her, either. I'm getting a little desperate."

The first old guy said, "Well, maybe I can help you find her. What does she look like?"

The second old guy replied, "She's 27 years old, tall, with red hair, blue eyes, long legs, and a big bust. She's wearing short shorts. What does your wife look like?"

"Never mind; let's look for yours first."

*   *   *

Retirement must be wonderful. I mean, you can suck in your stomach for only so long.

—BURT REYNOLDS

*   *   *

Two old men got to talking.

"You know, I can hardly remember anything. Things that happened just yesterday seem to have vanished from the memory banks in the old noodle," said the first.

The second answered, "I know what you mean. I can't recall the last time I had noodles, and I haven't been able to find my bank."

*   *   *

*The future will soon be
a thing of the past.*

—GEORGE CARLIN

*   *   *

On their 50th anniversary, Mike and Bev visited the bench in the park where he had proposed to her all those years before. Just remembering the romantic scene had them both feeling amorous, and they began making out on the bench like a couple of teenagers. Eventually, Mike said, "Bev, let's go home and make love."

Bev replied, "You'll have to pick one or the other, because I can't do both!"

*   *   *

No one even knows how many years Pete had been a sailor before he started to go a little dingy.

*   *   *

Great Expectations

When I was young, I thought that getting old meant that you had to repent for all the "bad" stuff you did when you were young. But now that I am old, I find that those are my best memories!

* * *

He's so old that when he orders a three-minute egg, they ask for the money up front.

—MILTON BERLE

* * *

Two women were talking about their handsome new neighbor in the senior home.

"He dresses so well."

"And so quickly!"

* * *

The most popular guy in the senior village is the retired carpenter. He still has all of his tools, and they really come in handy... opening pill bottles.

* * *

Q & A

· · · · ·

Q. What's the best-selling used
vehicle make for senior citizens?

A. An Oldsmobile

"Where is my Sunday paper?" the irate customer calling the newspaper office loudly demanded.

"Ma'am," said the newspaper employee, "today is Saturday. The Sunday paper is not delivered until tomorrow."

There was quite a long pause on the other end of the phone.... "So that's why no one was at church today."

* * *

The Brown family had a wonderful dog. They loved that dog, which had been with them for eight years, but Mrs. Brown finally had to insist that her husband take the dog and find him a new home. Mr. Brown wasn't happy about this and demanded to know the reason why.

"He keeps trying to drag Grandpa out back and bury him," Mrs. Brown explained.

* * *

One good thing about being older is that no one expects you to go running into a burning building.

$$* \quad * \quad *$$

You know you're old when you order a Sex on the Beach and ask if it comes with sunscreen.

GREAT ACCOMPLISHMENTS THROUGH THE AGES

3: Not peeing your pants

5: Starting kindergarten

16: Having a driver's license

18: Being able to vote

21: Being able to drink

65: Being able to retire

75: Having a driver's license

80: Not peeing your pants

One day, Marge told her husband she was worried that she was losing her memory.

"Look on the bright side," he suggested. "You'll meet someone new every day!"

✳   ✳   ✳

It takes a long time to become young.

—IRISH PROVERB

✳   ✳   ✳

The neighborhood had to do an intervention on the little old lady across the street. She was up to one new cat adoption a day.

✳   ✳   ✳

One evening, an old farmer in Florida decided to go down to the pond on his land. He grabbed a five-gallon bucket to bring back some fruit from the nearby trees. As he neared the pond, he heard voices

shouting and laughing with glee. As he came closer, he saw that a bunch of young women were skinny-dipping in his pond.

Once he made the women aware of his presence, they all went to the deeper water. One of the women shouted to him, "We're not coming out until you leave!"

The old man frowned, "I didn't come down here to watch you ladies swim naked or to make you get out of the pond naked." Holding the bucket up he said, "I'm here to feed the alligator."

* * *

You can live to be a hundred if you give up all the things that make you want to live to be a hundred.

—WOODY ALLEN

* * *

An Idea to Chew Over

An older man lost 50 pounds. At his book club, everyone was dying to know what his secret was. He just smiled and said, "Oh, it was really pretty easy, but I don't really want to talk about the secret."

After the meeting, one of the other members approached him again. "Please, Joe, I'm desperate to get these extra pounds off. Can't you just let me in on your secret?"

"Well, okay, but you have to promise not to tell anyone. I was really struggling, but then I heard on a talk show that you have to stop eating late at night, so now I just take my teeth out at 7:00. Works like a charm!"

* * *

Q & A

· · · · ·

Q: How many grannies does it take to change a lightbulb?

A: Two. One to change the bulb, and one to change the subject when the other starts talking about how it reminds her of hot flashes.

No matter what religion you belonged to during most of your lifetime, you eventually reach the age where Catholicism starts looking good just for the bingo.

*   *   *

A woman went for her first mammogram late in life. "I'm so excited!" she told the technician.

"Really? About a mammogram?"

"Yes! I've been waiting my whole life for someone to want to see me naked on film."

*   *   *

Larry explained to his dad, who was very hard of hearing, that his doctor wanted him to avoid all unnecessary stress. Then Larry found his dad throwing away all his doctor's bills unopened.

"These have been giving me too much stress for years," the dad said.

*   *   *

Just remember, once you're over the hill you begin to pick up speed.

—CHARLES M. SCHULZ

* * *

No one's claiming that seniors drive slowly, but the speed limit signs in the retirement community have been replaced by ones that say, "Hurry up, Grandma!"

* * *

The early bird might catch a worm, but some people have been around long enough to open their own bait shop!

* * *

One evening, Gladys got to pondering. "I don't know why they call it a 'will,'" she said. "My kids, who think I'm leaving them money, are going to find out it's a 'won't.'"

* * *

Joseph joined a new fraternity for senior citizens with high cholesterol. It's called Omega-3 Omega-3 Omega-3.

Definition from the old folks dictionary—cell phone: what you do when the buttons don't work anymore.

Mistaken Identity

An elderly woman was taking her turn driving during a vacation with her husband, when she got pulled over by a highway patrol officer.

"Ma'am, did you know you were speeding?" The woman, hard of hearing, turned to her husband and asked, "What did he say?" The old man yelled, "He says you were speeding!"

The officer asked, "May I see your license?" Again the woman asked her husband what was said, and her husband yelled back the response, "He needs to see your license!"

After the woman handed over her license, the officer remarked, "I see you are from a small town in Arkansas where I dated the world's most cantankerous woman."

The woman turned to her husband and asked, "What did he say?" The old man yelled back, "He says he thinks he knows you!"

* * *

*Inflation is when you pay
15 dollars for the 10 dollar
haircut you used to get for
5 dollars when you had hair.*

—SAM EWING

* * *

MOVIES FOR SENIORS

. . . .

- *Drawablanca*
- *The Silence of the Lambs when My Hearing Aid's Turned Off*
- *Some Like It Lukewarm*
- *Raiders of the Lost Car Keys*
- *Forrest Grumpy*
- *Dances with Walkers*
- *Mutiny at the Bingo Hall*
- *Guess What's Coming Up—Dinner!*

You know you're old when drinking too much last night doesn't give you a hangover... last night gives you a hangover all by itself.

$$* \quad * \quad *$$

Looking for writing paper, an older gentleman walked into a department store and approached an attractive young store clerk. "Excuse me, Miss," he asked, "do you keep stationery?"

"Usually until the last few seconds, then I go crazy."

$$* \quad * \quad *$$

When I was a kid I used to see two movies for five dollars. Now I've got a $2,000 flat-screen TV, and what do I see? Those same old movies.

$$* \quad * \quad *$$

The best way to keep looking young is to hang out with older people.

* * *

A woman's face had been severely burned in an accident and required skin grafting. Because she didn't have any skin of her own that was suitable, her husband lovingly offered himself as a donor. The doctor found what he needed on the spouse's buttocks. The couple decided that the details of the graft would remain a secret—after all, it was a little embarrassing.

After the wife was all healed, she once again expressed her appreciation to her husband. "How can I ever thank you enough?" she asked with great emotion. "Oh, my dear," he replied, smiling, "think nothing of it. I'll get all the thanks I need every time I see your miserable old mother kiss you on the cheek."

* * *

An elderly Polish man lay dying in his bed. While suffering the agonies of impending death, he suddenly smelled the aroma of his favorite pierogis with fried onions wafting up the stairs.

Gathering his remaining strength, he lifted himself from the bed. He gripped the railing with both hands and crawled downstairs. Were it not for death's agony, he would have thought himself already in heaven, for there in the kitchen, spread out upon waxed paper, were hundreds of his favorite pierogies.

Was this one final act of love from his wife of 60 years, seeing to it that he left this world a happy man? He threw himself toward the table, landing on his knees in a crumpled posture. His parched lips parted, and the wondrous taste of the pierogi was already in his mouth.

Suddenly, his wife smacked him with a wooden spoon.

"Back off!" she said. "Those are for the funeral."

$*$ $*$ $*$

I don't feel old. I don't feel anything until noon. That's when it's time for my nap.

—BOB HOPE

*   *   *

Why do so many retired folks want to be greeters at a store? Who wants a job where you can be replaced by a welcome mat?

*   *   *

Did You Forget Something?

Samantha decided that her grown children were old enough to write thank-you notes for the gifts they received without being reminded by her. As a result, an entire year went by without Grandfather receiving one single thank-you letter for the very generous checks he had included in his cards for his grandchildren's special occasions.

However, the following year, things changed dramatically.

"All my grandkids came over in person to thank me," Gramps declared to his best friend.

"How did you manage that?" questioned the friend.

"Oh, it was simple. This year I 'forgot' to sign their checks."

* * *

When I was younger, a "cooldown" meant a short walk after a long run; now, it means a cold shower after a hot flash.

* * *

The young man knows the rules, but the old man knows the exceptions.

—OLIVER WENDELL HOLMES SR.

* * *

Some people will never be too old to learn new ways of being stupid.

Q & A

· · · · ·

Q: What's a great thing about getting old?

A: You can date someone half your age, and it's totally legal.

You know you're getting older when you stop telling your grandkids about the school of hard knocks and start telling them to knock harder when they come over after school.

*   *   *

Three elderly gentlemen were talking about what their grandchildren would be saying about them 50 years from now.

"I'd like my grandchildren to say, 'He was successful in business,'" declared the first man.

"Fifty years from now," said the second, "I want them to say, 'He was a loyal family man.'"

Turning to the third gent, the first asked, "So what do you want them to say about you in 50 years?"

"Me?" the third man replied. "I want them to say, 'He certainly looks good for his age!'"

*   *   *

I don't plan to grow old gracefully; I plan to have face-lifts until my ears meet.

—RITA RUDNER

✳ ✳ ✳

He Should Have Wished for Wisdom

A man rubbed a bottle, and out came a genie, who offered him three wishes.

The man's first wish was to wake up on a bed full of money.

His second wish was to be the most powerful man in town.

And his third wish was to have a lovely wife 20 years his junior.

"Fine," said the genie. "When you wake up in the morning, your wishes will all be granted."

The man could hardly get to sleep that night, so great was his anticipation. But finally, he rolled over and was off to dreamland. When

he woke up the next morning, something was poking him in the back—he was sleeping on a bed of pennies. He went outside and found that his house had been moved way out to the countryside and was completely isolated. But the worst was when he saw his wife, and she looked the same as always. The man raced to the nearest mirror, and sure enough, he was 20 years older than he had been the day before.

* * *

Walter used to be a chemistry teacher. He still enjoys the odd experiment now and then. One of his favorites is taking beer, whiskey, bourbon, scotch, gin, vodka, and wine and turning it into urine.

* * *

John and Dan were having lunch at a diner. John said, "Hey, Dan, isn't your 60th anniversary coming up? What are you doing to celebrate?"

Dan replied, "I'm not sure. When we hit our 50th anniversary, my wife started walking two miles a day."

"Wow, she must be in great shape by walking that far!"

"Could be, but now I've got no idea where she is!"

* * *

When I was young, there was no respect for the youth. Now that I'm older, there's no respect for the aged. I missed it coming and going.

* * *

Mrs. Walker's doctor has put her on a new one-bite diet to help her lose weight and avoid foods that are bad for her. She can eat anything she wants as long as she takes one bite and, if it tastes good, she spits it out.

* * *

What's Up, Doc, and Does Medicare Cover It?

· · · · · · · · · · · · · · · · ·

An elderly gentleman was driving on the local freeway when his cell phone rang. It was his wife, who sounded frantic. She warned him to be on the lookout for a wayward driver.

"Sherman, please be very careful! I just heard on the radio that there's a driver on the freeway going in the wrong direction!"

"Margaret, you should call that radio station and give them an update. It's not just one driver. It's every single blasted car I pass!"

✳ ✳ ✳

You know you're getting old when you realize that 75 years ago, doctors who looked at people your age were called coroners.

✳ ✳ ✳

How Do You Keep Them All Straight?

I have become quite a fickle gal in my old age. In my younger days, I would see one or possibly two men a week, until I became serious about one of them. However, I tell you the truth, I'm pretty serious about all five of these guys I'm seeing right now.

Each morning, when I awake, Will Power gets me up out of bed.

Then I take a good long visit with John.

Unfortunately, before my visit with John is through, Charley Horse usually interrupts, and boy does he demand a lot of my attention.

Finally, he leaves, and then Arthur Itis shows up and keeps me company the rest of the day.

He's a real gadabout, though, always wanting to be noticed in one new joint or another.

After such a busy day, I am beat and ready to hit the hay with dear old Ben Gay.

* * *

The older I get, the better I used to be!

—LEE TREVINO

Mrs. Jenkins doesn't watch those TV news programs anymore. She gets enough bad news every morning from her talking bathroom scale.

You know you're old when you see the movie *Jurassic Park* and it brings back fond childhood memories.

*　　*　　*

A stubborn old fellow had been hard of hearing for a number of years, and his family had given up on him ever consenting to getting hearing aids.

Finally, however, he went to the doctor alone, and the doctor was successful in fitting him with a set of hearing aids that allowed the gentleman to hear at nearly 100 percent again.

He went back a month later to report to his doctor how pleased he was, and the doctor replied, "Your family must be delighted that you have your hearing back again."

The gentleman laughed and said, "Oh, I haven't breathed a word about it yet. I just sit around and listen to their conversations. I've changed my will three times already!"

*　　*　　*

BROADWAY MUSICALS FOR SENIORS

· · · · · · · · · · ·

- *Bedside Story*
- *Phantom of the Operation*
- *I'm Misérables*
- *A Funny Thing Happened on the Way to the Bathroom*
- *How to Succeed in Retirement Without Really Trying*
- *Get Off My Roof, You Fiddling Kids!*
- *Seven Widows for One Brother*
- *Cats...and More Cats*

I used to be concerned about the side effects of the medications I take. Now my favorite game is checking those side effects off as I get them.

✱   ✱   ✱

A husband and wife coming up on their 43rd anniversary were kissing on the couch, but the passion just wasn't there. Suddenly, they both stopped. After a few moments the husband said, "So, you couldn't think of anyone, either?"

*　　*　　*

B eing old is like being a dog. The high points of the day are scratching, peeing, and watching for the mailman.

*　　*　　*

You know you're getting old when the candles cost more than the cake.

—BOB HOPE

* * *

Charlotte took a jitterbug class and found out she couldn't do the turns and flips and splits she used to be able to do. The good news is, once she gets out of the hospital, she's planning to be on *Dancing with the Scars*.

* * *

A husband and wife attended a formal ball. Not too far away, the wife noticed an elegant older woman. She nudged her husband. "That woman's face looks so familiar, but I just can't place her name!"

The husband choked back his laughter and finally said, "That's a mirrored wall, honey."

* * *

AFTER SNOW WHITE RETIRED, SHE HIRED THE SEVEN SENIOR DWARFS

• •

- Nip
- Tuck
- Saggy
- Droopy
- Gassy
- Forgetful
- Dizzy

You know you're getting older when you open a fortune cookie and your fortune has a "use by" date.

*   *   *

Gramps: "When I was your age I could name all the presidents...in order."

Sonny: "When you were my age there were only five of them."

*   *   *

Old clockmakers never die, they just wind down.

* * *

Bob, a 70-year-old, extremely wealthy widower, showed up at the country club with a breathtakingly beautiful and very sexy 25-year-old blond who knocked everyone's socks off. She hung on Bob's arm and listened intently to his every word.

His buddies at the club were all aghast. At the first chance, they cornered him and asked, "Bob, how'd you get the trophy girlfriend?"

Bob replied, "Girlfriend? She's my wife!"

They were blown over. "So, how'd you persuade her to marry you?"

"I lied about my age," Bob replied.

"What, you told her you were only 50?"

Bob smiled and said, "No, I told her I was 90."

* * *

You know you're old if you can remember when instant photos, instant coffee, and instant mashed potatoes took minutes to make.

*   *   *

A diplomat is a man who always remembers a woman's birthday but never remembers her age.

—ROBERT FROST

*   *   *

Nothing makes gray hair more attractive than baldness.

* * *

A distraught senior citizen phoned her doctor's office. "Is it true that the medication you prescribed has to be taken for the rest of my life?"

"Yes, I'm afraid so," the doctor told her.

There was a moment of silence before the senior lady replied, "Just how serious is my condition? This prescription is marked 'NO REFILLS'."

* * *

I have everything now that I had 20 years ago, except now it's all lower.

—GYPSY ROSE LEE

* * *

How come stores don't have mannequins that look like old people? The worst mannequins are the ones with blank heads. There are no eyes for glasses, no ears for hearing aids, no nose for an oxygen hose, and no mouth to complain that there's no mannequins that look like old people.

*   *   *

There was once a man and woman who had been married for more than 60 years. They'd shared everything, they'd talked about everything, and they kept no secrets from each other. Well, no secrets other than the shoebox the old woman kept in the top of her closet that her husband was never to open or ask her about.

For all of these years, he had never thought much about that box, but one day the little old woman got very sick, and the doctor said she would not recover. In trying to sort out their affairs, the little old man took down the shoebox out of the closet and brought it to his wife's bedside. She agreed that it was time that he should know what was in the box.

When he opened it, the man found two crocheted doilies and a stack of money totaling $25,000. He asked her about the contents.

"When we were to be wed," she said, "my grandmother told me the secret of a happy marriage was never to argue. She told me

that if I ever got angry with you, I should just keep quiet and crochet a doily."

The little old man was so moved he had to fight back tears. Only two precious doilies were in the box. She had only been angry with him twice in all those years of living and loving. He almost burst with happiness.

"Honey," he said, "that explains the doilies, but what about all of this money? Where did it come from?"

"Oh," she said, "that's the money I made from selling the doilies."

* * *

Things are so much more advanced these days than when I was a kid—flat-screen TVs, phones that take pictures, and my state-of-the-art washer/dryer. It talks. This morning, it told me where the missing socks are.

* * *

An elderly woman decided to prepare her will and told her preacher she had two final requests. First, she wanted to be cremated, and second, she wanted her ashes scattered over the grocery store.

"The grocery store?" the preacher exclaimed. "Why the grocery store?"

She replied, "I want to be sure my daughters will visit me twice a week."

＊　　＊　　＊

Lionel: "There's nothing worse than being old and broke, son."

Lionel Jr.: "Sure there is—being young and broke with an old dad."

* * *

Retirement at 65 is ridiculous. When I was 65, I still had pimples.

—GEORGE BURNS

* * *

Married men don't live longer than single men—it just seems like it.

* * *

People say that life really begins at 40. Well, that may be true, but it really begins to start showing after 50.

* * *

You know you're old when you can see your freckles despite having poor eyesight... and then you realize they're liver spots.

*   *   *

Greedy Little Toad

A grandpa was walking through the woods with his grandson when they came to a small pond. The grandpa said, "Let's wait, and maybe we'll hear a frog croak."

The grandson asked, "Grandpa, would you croak?"

The grandpa did his best croak, but the boy didn't seem impressed. He kept asking his grandpa if he would croak. The grandpa finally asked, "Why do you keep asking me if I will croak?"

The grandson replied, "Dad told me when you croak, we'll get a lot of money."

*   *   *

True terror is to wake up one morning and discover that your high school class is running the country.

—KURT VONNEGUT

*　　*　　*

Mr. Wilson still has a full deck; he just shuffles a lot slower now.

*　　*　　*

Who needs a gym membership? At this age, a person can work up a sweat just trying to get the peanut butter sandwich unstuck from the roof of her mouth.

*　　*　　*

SENIOR DEFINITION
· · · · · · · · · · · · · · · · ·
App: half of a Golden Delicious

Nellie was sitting in front of her computer, staring at the screen but not doing anything else. Her grandson couldn't figure out what she was doing, so he asked.

Nellie explained: "I need to move the computer to the rear of my desk so I can find my pen. I hit 'backup,' and now I'm waiting for it to back up."

*   *   *

Gertie went to the gym to lift weights, and the trainer asked if she needed a spotter. "No," Gertie said, "I have plenty of spots already."

* * *

I never think of the future.
It comes soon enough.

—ALBERT EINSTEIN

* * *

If necessity is the mother of invention, how come so much unnecessary junk has been invented in my lifetime?

* * *

Jack went to visit his great-aunt when she finally retired, and he barely recognized her. "I guess old bookkeepers really do lose their figures," he said.

* * *

But Would You Recommend Him?

Two elderly friends were golfing one Saturday, when one mentioned he was going to be fitted for dentures the following Monday.

"Oh really, who's your dentist?" asked his friend, Harry.

"Dr. Tillman, do you know him?"

Harry was never one to say a bad word about anyone if he could help it, so he thought for a moment. "Yes, Davy, I know him. He is the dentist who fitted me for dentures about four years ago."

"You don't say," Davy remarked. "Did he do a good job?"

"Well, I'll tell you the truth, I was out here last week, and a fellow on the ninth hole hooked a shot something terrible. The ball hit me and knocked the wind right out of me. That was the first time since Dr. Tillman put my dentures in that I didn't notice how much they hurt."

SENIOR ROCK BANDS

- Grateful Not Dead
- Moody and Blue
- No-Fat Cream
- Blood, Sweat, and Call the Doctor
- Crosby, Stills, Nash, and Old
- Creedence Cardiac Revival
- The Door's Stuck
- Burp, Wind, and Farting
- Can't Eat Red Hot Chili Peppers
- Alice in Chair
- The Velvet Underwear

I don't mind having arthritis. It gives me a good excuse when the guy who cut me off pulls up and wants to know why I gave him the finger.

* * *

A senior citizen to his 87-year-old buddy: "So I hear you're getting married?"

"Yep!"

"This woman, is she good looking?"

"Not really."

"Is she a good cook?"

"Naw, she can't cook too well."

"Does she have lots of money?"

"No, poor as a church mouse."

"Is she good in bed?"

"I don't know."

"Why in the world do you want to marry her, then?"

"She can still drive at night."

* * *

An older man sat at the bus stop, looking incredibly sad. A young woman walked up to him and said, "Excuse me, sir, but is everything all right?"

"Well," he said slowly, "my wife ran off with my best friend last week."

"No wonder you look so blue!"

"Yeah, I really do miss him."

✳   ✳   ✳

Charlie was at his friend Richard's home for dinner. Richard preceded every request to his wife with endearing terms, calling her Sweetie, Sugar, Honey, Baby, and so on throughout the entire evening. When the wife left the dining room to prepare dessert, Charlie couldn't help but comment on it.

"Wow, Rich, this is really something. The affection you show you wife after what, 45 years? The way you keep calling her all those sweet names!"

"Oh, Charlie, please don't say anything," came the embarrassed reply. "I forgot her name years ago."

* * *

When you're young, "get lucky" means to have sex. For seniors, "get lucky" means to have sex without calling 911.

* * *

Grandchildren don't make a man feel old; it's the knowledge that he's married to a grandmother.

—G. NORMAN COLLIE

* * *

Retirement: Twice the time, half the money.

* * *

An 81-year-old woman went in to get her first tattoo. As the tattoo artist worked the needle over the intricate design, she found herself more and more curious, until she couldn't help but ask the woman, "Why are you getting a tattoo this late in life?"

The old woman grinned and replied, "Well, it's something I've wanted to do since my 50s, but I figured if I waited, we could just incorporate the sagging into the design!"

* * *

What Did He Ever Do?

An aged farmer and his wife were walking past their pigpen when the old woman began to reflect that soon the couple would be married 50 years.

"Let's do something special, Clovis. Let's invite all our friends and family over and kill a nice fat pig."

The old farmer stopped in his tracks and looked at his wife as if she had finally lost her mind. "That just doesn't seem quite right, Myrtle. Why should we punish one of our finest pigs over a mistake we made 50 years ago?"

* * *

Surely the consolation of old age is finding out how few things are worth worrying over.

—DOROTHY DIX

*　*　*

What a Way to Go!

A 97-year-old man went to his doctor to get a physical.

A few days later the doctor noticed his patient walking down the street, grinning from ear to ear, with a dazzling young lady on his arm. The doctor called the man aside and said, "Mr. Adams, what are you doing?"

The man replied, "Just doing exactly what you said, Doc! 'Get a hot mamma, and please be cheerful.'"

To which the doctor exclaimed, "I didn't say that at all. I said you've got a heart murmur, please be careful!"

*　*　*

The only way to keep your health is to eat what you don't want, drink what you don't like, and do what you'd rather not.

—MARK TWAIN

*　*　*

Have you heard about the new amusement park for seniors? The roller coasters go five miles an hour and leave the turn signal on for the whole ride.

*　*　*

Jane came out to the living room with her hair in curlers.

"I just set my hair," she told her husband.

"Great! What time will it go off?"

*　*　*

Emma and Shelley, friends since they served together in the WACs, were commiserating about their age over some take-out Chinese food. Emma cracked open her fortune cookie and read this advice: "The only way to achieve inner peace is to finish what you've started."

There was a pause, then both women burst out laughing.

"I've got a box of chocolates with my name on it!" crowed Shelley.

"And I've got half a bottle of single-malt scotch to wash it down with!" finished Emma.

*   *   *

In the middle of a fight, Mike asked his wife, "You've been making me look like such a fool for 37 years. Why must you do that?"

She serenely replied, "I don't do anything—you're a do-it-yourselfer!"

*   *   *

The Latest Thing...

Every day, Mark saw his grandmother do the same thing: She would go outside, stand quietly with her head tilted as if she were listening to something, then walk from tree to tree to tree. Finally, one morning he followed her to ask, "Grandma, what are you doing?"

"Well, I heard that the latest thing was to follow the tweets...."

* * *

Expiration Dates Are Depressing

· · · · · · · · · · · · · · · ·

Groups of Americans were traveling by tour bus through Holland. As they stopped at a cheese farm, a young guide led them through the process of cheese making, explaining that this cheese used goat's milk.

Then she showed the group a lovely hillside where many goats were grazing. "These," she explained, "are the older goats, put out to pasture when they no longer produce."

Curious, she asked the group, "What do you do in America with your old goats?"

One spry old gentleman answered, "They send us on bus tours!"

* * *

You know you're getting old when you get winded while asking your doctor why you get winded.

* * *

A local clown specializes in birthday parties for seniors. He brings two tanks: one with helium for the balloons, and one with oxygen for the guests.

* * *

Perhaps one has to be very old before one learns how to be amused rather than shocked.

—PEARL S. BUCK

* * *

A woman enjoyed a private moment with her granddaughter just before the grand-daughter's wedding.

"Grandma, do you have any last-minute advice for me?"

"Well, Jane, do you love him?"

"I really do!"

"Then you'd better watch out."

"Why would you say something like that, Grandma?"

"Because love may be blind, but marriage is a real eye-opener!"

* * *

Gertrude has come to the conclusion that it is a lot easier to get older than it is to get wiser.

*　*　*

THE BEACH BOYS (OR SHOULD THAT BE THE LITTLE OLD BEACH MEN?) SING THEIR SENIOR HITS
. . . .

- (I Remember Feelin' Those) Good Vibrations
- In My Room (at the Home)
- Wouldn't It Be Nice if We Were Younger
- Little Deuce Toupee
- I'm Dating a Little Old Lady from Pasadena
- All Summer Long (if I'm Lucky)
- (Creamed) Kokomo

You know you're old when you tell the grandkids that you've just been on a pilgrimage, and they think you meant on *The Mayflower.*

*   *   *

Old age is 15 years older than I am.

—OLIVER WENDELL HOLMES

*   *   *

Everyone in the family is more than happy to give Grandma a ride anywhere she wants to go at just about anytime she wants. That's because none of them wants to be on the road when she's behind the wheel.

*   *   *

You know you're going through menopause when all of your clothes are sweat clothes.

Wesley's grandkids keep trying to convince him that computers will replace phone books. "Horse hockey!" Wesley replies. "Show me a computer that I can sit on to see over the steering wheel, stand on to reach the back of the cupboard, and swing to send a spider to bug heaven."

*   *   *

Old Gus has taken so many antibiotics that with one sneeze, he can cure the patient sitting next to him.

* * *

Doctor Bloom was known for miraculous cures for arthritis. He had a waiting room full of people when a little old lady, completely bent over in half, shuffled in slowly, leaning on her cane. When the lady's turn came, she went into the examination room and, amazingly, emerged only a few minutes later walking completely erect with her head held high.

One woman still in the waiting room said, "It's a miracle! You walked in bent in half, and now you're walking erect. What did that doctor do?"

She answered, "Miracle, shmiricle. He gave me a longer cane."

* * *

Life is a moderately good play with a badly written third act.

—TRUMAN CAPOTE

*　　*　　*

There's a new commercial for something to serve your kids when they visit. The ad's slogan? "Guilt: It's what's for dinner."

*　　*　　*

Q & A
· · · · ·

Q: How many little old ladies does it take to change a lightbulb?

A: Three. One to change the bulb, one to complain about how they don't make bulbs like they used to, and one to call all of their friends to let them know the bulb died.

On his wedding day, Tom asked his grandfather if he had any sage advice.

"Not really," came the reply. "Being married is incredibly wonderful most of the time."

"Then why do you look so sad, Grandpa?"

"Because the rest of the time, you're still married!"

* * *

Malcolm knew Grandpa wasn't doing too well when his doctor told him to stop buying green bananas.

* * *

Good, Clean Living?

A woman saw a decrepit, little old man sitting quietly in a rocking chair on his porch, and she had a question for him.

"I couldn't help noticing how content you look," she said. "What's your secret for a long, happy life?"

"Well," he began, "I smoke three packs of cigarettes a day. I also drink about a gallon of whiskey a week, eat all the fatty foods I want, and I never exercise."

"That's incredible!" the woman exclaimed. "If you don't mind me asking, how old are you?"

"I'll be 32 next week," the fellow answered.

* * *

One nice thing about going into the swimming pool when you're 60 . . . you don't have to worry about being more wrinkled when you come out.

* * *

Old attorneys never die, they just lose their appeal.

* * *

One bad thing about dinner at the nursing home: When friends are absent, it's hard to tell who's checked out for dinner, and who's just checked out.

* * *

Gladys and Madge were having coffee and talking about their love lives.

"What are you complaining for, Madge?" Gladys asked. "You've been married to the same guy for 48 years. You've got three lovely, grown children."

"Yeah," Madge replied, "but if Walter didn't toss and turn in his sleep, we'd never have had any of them."

* * *

Seniors: We have control over our destinies—our bladders, not so much.

* * *

*Whatever wrinkles I got,
I enjoyed getting them.*

—AVA GARDNER

* * *

Warren looks on the bright side. "My pants keep sliding down. I've got no hair, so my baseball cap keeps flipping around. Half of my teeth are gold. It took me 60 years, but I'm finally hip again."

* * *

Jackson's calmed down over the years. "I had a bit of a jealous streak when I was younger. Now, I really don't care where my wife goes, as long as I don't have to go with her."

* * *

A couple was checking into a hotel for a second honeymoon on their 45th anniversary. The desk clerk asked if they'd prefer a room with a bathtub or a shower.

"What's the difference?" the husband asked.

The desk clerk replied, "Well, with a tub, you sit down."

* * *

I was thinking about how people seem to read the Bible a whole lot more as they get older. Then it dawned on me . . . they're cramming for their final exam.

—GEORGE CARLIN

*   *   *

Agnes used to buy health food to help her live longer, but she quit when she heard people can die from natural causes.

*   *   *

Ralph is so lucky. He has a big-screen TV, a remote control, and a wife of 50 years. And they all still work.

*   *   *

A retired man volunteered to entertain at a nursing home. He told jokes and sang some funny songs at patients' bedsides.

As he was leaving, he usually said, "I hope you get better."

One day, an elderly gentleman replied, "I hope you get better, too."

Dating someone younger than your kids can be a shock to your heart...not to mention to your kids.

Old age comes at a bad time.

—SAN BANDUCCI

* * *

Janet looked up from the newspaper. "I don't know why they keep calling these the 'Golden Years.'"

"What would you rather they call them?" asked her husband.

"Oh, I don't know. Maybe the 'Surgical-Grade Titanium Years'?"

* * *

When Hazel was young, she used to search for potatoes that looked like the heads of famous people. As she got older, she quit when she noticed that all of the potatoes were starting to look like her.

* * *

Hospital regulations require a wheelchair for patients being discharged. A student nurse found one elderly gentleman—already dressed and sitting on the bed with a suitcase at his feet—who insisted he didn't need her help to leave the hospital.

After a chat about rules being rules, the man reluctantly let the nurse wheel him to the elevator. On the way down, she asked if his wife were meeting him.

"I don't know," he said. "She's still upstairs in the bathroom changing out of her hospital gown."

A doctor has a stethoscope up to a man's chest. The man asks, "Doc, how do I stand?" The doctor says, "That's what puzzles me!"

—HENNY YOUNGMAN

* * *

I knew I was getting old when my grand-daughter said, "Look, Grandma, you've got angel wings." Before I could set her straight, she began flipping the flab under my arms. "See? These wings."

* * *

There's a wedding chapel in town that caters to senior couples getting married by help-ing them feel like youngsters again. For an extra tip, the minister hires a guy to dress like the bride's father and threaten the groom with a shotgun.

* * *

After she misplaced and hunted up her keys for the fifth time in the same day, Patty was finally ready to go out to dinner with her husband. On the way out the door, she commented, "Sometimes, I really think I've lost my mind."

"It wouldn't surprise me," muttered her husband.

"What did you just say?" asked Patty, outraged.

"I said it wouldn't surprise me—you've given me a piece of it every day for the past 40 years now!"

*   *   *

Eldon never has any trouble with door-to-door solicitors.

By the time he gets all of the locks unlocked to open the door, they've been gone for half an hour.

*   *   *

The Pearly Gates

After a long illness, a woman died and arrived at the gates of heaven. While she was waiting for Saint Peter to greet her, she peeked through the gates themselves. She saw a beautiful banquet table. Sitting all around were her parents and all the other people she had loved and who had died before her. They saw her and began calling greetings to her.

When Saint Peter came by, the woman said to him, "This is such a wonderful place! How do I get in?" "You have to spell a word," Saint Peter told her. "Which word?" the woman asked. "Love." The woman correctly spelled "love," and Saint Peter welcomed her into heaven.

Some time later, Saint Peter came to the woman and asked her to watch the gates of heaven for him. While she was guarding them, her husband arrived. "I'm surprised to see you," the woman said. "How have you been?"

"Oh, I've been doing pretty well since you died," her husband told her. "I married the beautiful young nurse who took care of you while you were ill. And then I won the lottery. I sold the little house you and I lived in and bought a big mansion. My wife and I traveled all around the world. We were on vacation, and today I went skiing. I fell and hit my head, and here I am. How do I get in?"

"You have to spell a word," the woman told him. "Which word?" her husband asked.

"Antediluvian."

* * *

A New Wine for Seniors

California vintners in the Napa Valley area, which primarily produces Pinot Blanc, Pinot Noir, and Pinot Grigio wines, have developed a new hybrid grape that is expected to reduce the number of trips older people have to make to the bathroom during the night.

The new wine will be marketed as Pinot More.

* * *

Life's tragedy is that we get old too soon and wise too late.

—BENJAMIN FRANKLIN

*   *   *

Said one friend to another, "I feel like I've lost my mind!"

"Don't worry," replied the first. "It won't be long before you forget why you needed it."

*   *   *

You know the economy is bad when Grandma calls to say, "I've fallen, and I found three dollars in change under the couch!"

*   *   *

At Sammy's age, the last person he wants to hear say, "But wait . . . there's more!" is a doctor holding his X-rays.

Two 90-year-old women, Rose and Barb, had been friends all of their lives.

When Rose fell ill, Barb visited her every day. As death seemed to be moving closer, Barb said, "Rose, we both loved playing women's softball all our lives, and we played all through high school. Please do me one favor: When you get to heaven, somehow you have to let me know if there's women's softball there."

Rose agreed to do all that would be in her power and then passed on.

At midnight a few nights later, Barb was awakened from a sound sleep by a blinding flash of white light and a voice calling her name.

"Who is it?" asked Barb, sitting up suddenly.

"Barb—it's me, Rose. I have good news and bad news. The good news is that there's softball in heaven. Better yet, all of our old buddies who died before us are here, too. Better than that, we're all young again. It's always springtime, and it never rains or snows. And

best of all, we can play softball all we want, and we never get tired."

"That's fantastic," said Barb. "It's beyond my wildest dreams! So what's the bad news?"

"You're pitching Tuesday."

∗　　∗　　∗

Dennis started out with nothing, and with many years of careful planning, it seems he still has most of it.

*   *   *

A grandfather is a man who can't understand how his idiot son could have such brilliant and beautiful children.

*   *   *

Albert used to be an economist, but you might say that he never really retired. His hairline is in recession, his stomach is showing signs of hyperinflation, and if anyone mentions either of these things to him, it puts him into a great depression.

*   *   *

Roscoe complained, "We have the highest standard of living in the world. Now I just wish I could afford it. "

*Age mellows some people;
others it makes rotten.*

—ANONYMOUS

* * *

Christine was thinking about getting her tongue pierced. That little stud would be a great place to hook a chain so she didn't lose her dentures anymore.

* * *

Have you seen the new social media site for seniors? It's called Faceliftbook.

* * *

When Rex was younger, he used to do push-ups, sit-ups, and pull-ups every morning to get in shape. He still does them, but now it's to put on his shirt, pants, and shoes.

A Quiet Man

Mildred, the church gossip and self-appointed monitor of the church's morals, kept sticking her nose into other people's business. Several members didn't approve of her extracurricular activities, but they feared her enough to keep their silence.

Mildred made a mistake, however, when she accused Henry, a new member, of being an alcoholic after she saw his old pickup parked in front of the town's only bar one afternoon. She emphatically told Henry in the presence of other church members that she'd seen it and knew what he was doing.

Henry, a man of few words, stared at her for a moment and just turned and walked away. He didn't explain, defend, or deny. He said nothing.

Later that evening, Henry quietly parked his pickup in front of Mildred's house, walked home . . . and left it there all night.

*   *   *

When you get old and your eyesight blurs, forget the glasses, just try weaker drinks.

* * *

Things weren't turning out quite the way Chester intended. Working hard all his life and investing his money well, he'd hoped one day to retire and be a little pampered. However, he didn't realize that by now he'd also be wearing them.

* * *

The irony of aging: Just when you start to get it together mentally, your body starts to fall apart.

* * *

Now that Mr. Anderson was retired, he finally had the time to read as much as he wanted to. The only problem he had was finding enough time to find his reading glasses.

* * *

The folks at the senior center had to quit talking about Social Security because it made them antisocial and insecure.

* * *

A health-care expert was addressing a large audience in Tampa:

"The material we put into our stomachs is enough to have killed most of us sitting here, years ago. Red meat is awful. Soft drinks corrode your stomach lining. Chinese food is loaded with MSG. High-fat diets can be disastrous, and none of us realizes the long-term harm caused by the germs in our drinking water. But there is one thing that is the most dangerous of all. Can anyone here tell me which food causes us the most grief and suffering for years after eating it?"

After several seconds of quiet, a 75-year-old man in the front row raised his hand and softly said, "Wedding cake."

* * *

Great-Aunt Lucille had played the violin for over 50 years, so her family was surprised when she suddenly decided to take up the cello. "It's harder to misplace," she explained.

* * *

IF SENIORS HAD OUR OWN TV NETWORK, WE'D BE WATCHING:

- *Pimp My Walker*
- *Saturday Afternoon Live*
- *The New Adventures of Old What's-Her-Name*
- *How I Met Your Great-Grandmother*
- *Law & Order: Get Those Kids Off My Lawn Unit*
- *Doctor Who...Who?...WHO?*
- *The Price Is Right if I Can Use a Coupon*